Animal Colors
Yellow Animals

by Christina Leaf

BLASTOFF! READERS

BELLWETHER MEDIA • MINNEAPOLIS, MN

Note to Librarians, Teachers, and Parents:

Blastoff! Readers are carefully developed by literacy experts and combine standards-based content with developmentally appropriate text.

Level 1 provides the most support through repetition of high-frequency words, light text, predictable sentence patterns, and strong visual support.

Level 2 offers early readers a bit more challenge through varied simple sentences, increased text load, and less repetition of high-frequency words.

Level 3 advances early-fluent readers toward fluency through increased text and concept load, less reliance on visuals, longer sentences, and more literary language.

Level 4 builds reading stamina by providing more text per page, increased use of punctuation, greater variation in sentence patterns, and increasingly challenging vocabulary.

Level 5 encourages children to move from "learning to read" to "reading to learn" by providing even more text, varied writing styles, and less familiar topics.

Whichever book is right for your reader, Blastoff! Readers are the perfect books to build confidence and encourage a love of reading that will last a lifetime!

This edition first published in 2019 by Bellwether Media, Inc.

No part of this publication may be reproduced in whole or in part without written permission of the publisher. For information regarding permission, write to Bellwether Media, Inc., Attention: Permissions Department, 6012 Blue Circle Drive, Minnetonka, MN 55343.

Library of Congress Cataloging-in-Publication Data

Names: Leaf, Christina, author.
Title: Yellow Animals / by Christina Leaf.
Description: Minneapolis, MN : Bellwether Media, Inc., 2019. | Series: Blastoff! Readers. Animal Colors | Audience: Ages 5 to 8. | Audience: K to Grade 3. | Includes bibliographical references and index.
Identifiers: LCCN 2018001077 (print) | LCCN 2018005284 (ebook) | ISBN 9781626178328 (hardcover : alk. paper) | ISBN 9781681035734 (ebook)
Subjects: LCSH: Animals--Color--Juvenile literature. | Yellow--Juvenile literature.
Classification: LCC QL767 (ebook) | LCC QL767 .L443 2019 (print) | DDC 591.47/2--dc23
LC record available at https://lccn.loc.gov/2018001077

Editor: Betsy Rathburn   Designer: Jeffrey Kollock

Printed in the United States of America, North Mankato, MN

Table of Contents

Warning Colors

Where do you see yellow? Many road signs are yellow. They tell drivers to watch out.

fire salamander

Yellow Around You

bananas

daffodils

crossing signs

Yellow animals say watch out, too! Some are deadly. The blue-ringed octopus is **venomous**.

Yellow boxfish look friendly. But they are deadly to **predators**.

Bold stripes call out bumblebees' sharp **stingers**.

Attention Seekers

Some animals are yellow for attention. Female goldfinches like yellow males. Brighter is better!

13

Smart Hiders

Other yellow animals want to be hidden. Cheetahs slink unseen through tall grasses.

Eastern box turtles
hide among leaves.
Yellow spots look like
sunlight on their shells.

Goldenrod crab spiders hide from **prey** on flower petals.

Eyelash pit vipers hang from banana trees. These yellow snakes blend in!

Glossary

predators

animals that hunt
other animals
for food

stingers

sharp body parts
that may give
off venom

prey

animals that are
hunted by other
animals for food

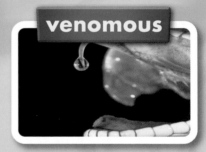

venomous

able to create a
deadly substance
called venom

To Learn More

AT THE LIBRARY

Adamson, Heather. *Yellow*. Minneapolis, Minn.: Bullfrog Books, 2014.

Borth, Teddy. *Yellow Animals*. Minneapolis, Minn.: Abdo Group, 2015.

Perish, Patrick. *Bumblebees*. Minneapolis, Minn.: Bellwether Media, 2019.

ON THE WEB
Learning more about yellow animals is as easy as 1, 2, 3.

1. Go to www.factsurfer.com.

2. Enter "yellow animals" into the search box.

3. Click the "Surf" button and you will see a list of related web sites.

With factsurfer.com, finding more information is just a click away.

Index

The images in this book are reproduced through the courtesy of: Matthew W Keefe, front cover; Fedor Sidorov, front cover, pp. 2, 3, 22, 23, 24; kotoffei, pp. 4-21 (brushstrokes); Martin Prochazkacz, pp. 4-5; Alexander Mazurkevich, p. 5 (bottom left); Drakuliren, p. 5 (bottom center); Titikul_B, p. 5 (bottom right); kaschibo, pp. 6-7; Suwat Sirivutcharungchit, pp. 8-9; Gorlov-KV, pp. 10-11; Gerald Marella, pp. 12-13; Ivan Mateev, pp. 14-15; Jay Ondreicka, pp. 16-17; Vitalii Hulai, pp. 18-19; Thomas Marent/ Visuals Unlimited, Inc./ Getty Images, pp. 20-21; Viju Jose, p. 22 (top left); Henrik Larsson, p. 22 (bottom left); Frank Reiser, p. 22 (top right); Joe McDonald, p. 22 (bottom right); Valerio Pardi, p. 24.

TRADITIONAL STORIES OF THE PLAINS NATIONS

BY MARIE POWELL

CONTENT CONSULTANT
Walter C. Fleming, PhD
Department Head and Professor, Native American Studies
Montana State University

Core Library

An Imprint of Abdo Publishing
abdopublishing.com

Cover image: Mandan flute player Keith Bear plays in
North Dakota near the Missouri River.

abdopublishing.com

Published by Abdo Publishing, a division of ABDO, PO Box 398166,
Minneapolis, Minnesota 55439. Copyright © 2018 by Abdo Consulting
Group, Inc. International copyrights reserved in all countries. No part of this
book may be reproduced in any form without written permission from the
publisher. Core Library™ is a trademark and logo of Abdo Publishing.

Printed in the United States of America, North Mankato, Minnesota
032017
092017

Cover Photo: Marilyn Angel Wynn/NativeStock
Interior Photos: Marilyn Angel Wynn/NativeStock, 1; Eye Ubiquitous/Universal Images Group/
Getty Images, 4–5; Zack Frank/Shutterstock Images, 7, 43; Pauline Webb/Eagle Butte News/AP
Images, 10–11; Red Line Editorial, 13, 30; MPI/Archive Photos/Getty Images, 14–15; Visions of
America/Universal Images Group/Getty Images, 17; Tom Reichner/Shutterstock Images, 18–19;
Susan Biddle/The Washington Post/Getty Images, 21; Michal Krakowiak/iStockphoto, 23; Robert
Cicchetti/Shutterstock Images, 24; Jose More/VWPics/AP Images, 26–27, 45; Viktar Malyshchyts/
Shutterstock Images, 29; Alex Wong/Getty Images News/Getty Images, 34–35; Sean Kilpatrick/The
Canadian Press/AP Images, 40; Mike Carroccetto/Getty Images News/Getty Images, 38–39

Editor: Arnold Ringstad
Imprint Designer: Maggie Villaume
Series Design Direction: Ryan Gale

Publisher's Cataloging-in-Publication Data

Names: Powell, Marie, author.
Title: Traditional stories of the Plains nations / by Marie Powell.
Description: Minneapolis, MN : Abdo Publishing, 2018. | Series: Native American
    oral histories | Includes bibliographical references and index.
Identifiers: LCCN 2016962141 | ISBN 9781532111754 (lib. bdg.) |
    ISBN 9781680789607 (ebook)
Subjects: LCSH: Indians of North America--Juvenile literature. | Indians of North
    America--Social life and customs--Juvenile literature. | Indian mythology--
    North America--Juvenile literature. | Indians of North America--Folklore--
    Juvenile literature.
Classification: DDC 979--dc23
LC record available at http://lccn.loc.gov/2016962141

CONTENTS

CHAPTER ONE

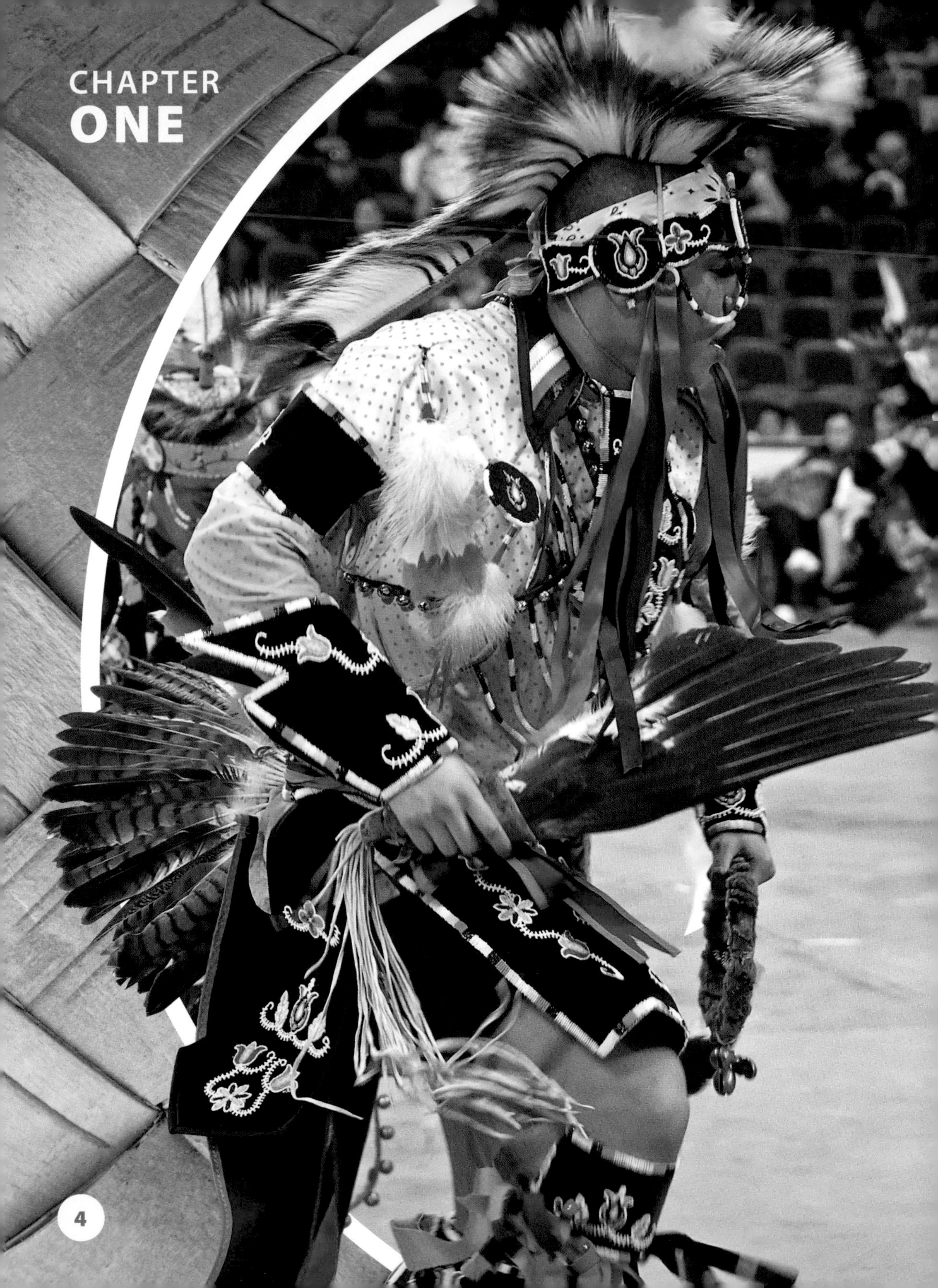

THE STORY PATH

I magine you are at a gathering of people in a school gym. The story begins with the sound of a drum. The clear, strong voice of the storyteller rings out. The words stretch back thousands of years across the rolling plains of North America.

The words take listeners into a world where animals share their stories. In these tales the land holds danger. But it is also the key to survival. Soon the listeners forget the hard gym floor. They share laughter and learning. Stories and ceremonies help the Plains Nations pass along their way of life.

Storytelling, dancing, and ceremonies are often held in community gathering places, such as school gyms or arenas.

PEOPLE OF THE PLAINS

West to east, the Plains region spans the area from the Rocky Mountains to the Mississippi River. North to south, it stretches from Canada to central Texas. Many types of grass, sage, and plants cover the region. Foothills and forests are found here too. The weather can be extreme. In the winter, temperatures can fall far below freezing. In the summer, they can rise to more than 90 degrees Fahrenheit (32°C).

More than 30 different nations live in this area. They include the Cree (Nei-yahw), the Siksika,

THE POWER OF THE WORD

Plains storytellers use their voices, faces, and body movements. A storyteller may clap or speak loudly or softly. He or she may make animal noises or imitate other natural sounds, such as wind. Some words also contain sounds from nature and animals. These words can have more than one meaning in a story. The stories often carry more meaning in their original languages than when they are translated.

The Black Hills of South Dakota and Wyoming lie within the Plains region.

the Mandan (Numakiki), and many others. For the Plains Nations, the landscape is bound to their oral traditions.

THE IMPORTANCE OF STORIES

Today's storytellers may be men or women, young or old. Often, the storyteller tells a traditional story the way he or she heard it told. Some storytellers may change stories to match new situations. These oral traditions are important in people's lives today.

Stories share information about the past. Some tell how the world was created. Some are about heroes or tricksters. Stories may warn people about seasonal danger. They may tell how to care for the land. A story may be told because it reminds the storyteller of problems people have lived through before. Stories can also help people think about how old traditions apply to life today.

STRAIGHT TO THE
SOURCE

Philomine Lakota (Hohwoju, Itazipacola, and
Oglala Lakota) and Stella Long (Choctaw) are modern
storytellers. In this article by writer Shannon Smith, they
explain how they think about their work:

> *"I have a big fear that a lot of these ceremonies will be
> forgotten. We have too much competition with the modern
> world," Philomine Lakota said. . . . The oral tradition is also how
> history was passed down through generations. With a written
> language developing later, words and memories were the best
> ways to transmit information. . . . "I don't always dig into the past
> because stories are out there now. And someday, what I tell will
> be history," [Stella] Long said. "That's what a man told me one
> time: 'Your stories are important. It's stories of today, but 20 years
> from now it's going to be history and people will be wanting to
> hear it.'"*

Source: Shannon Smith. "Native Storytellers Connect the
Past and the Future." *Native Daughters*. University of
Nebraska–Lincoln, n.d. Web. Accessed October 24, 2016.

What's the Big Idea?
Take a close look at this passage. How do the
storytellers think about modern storytelling? What
do they think remains important about stories
from the past?

CHAPTER TWO

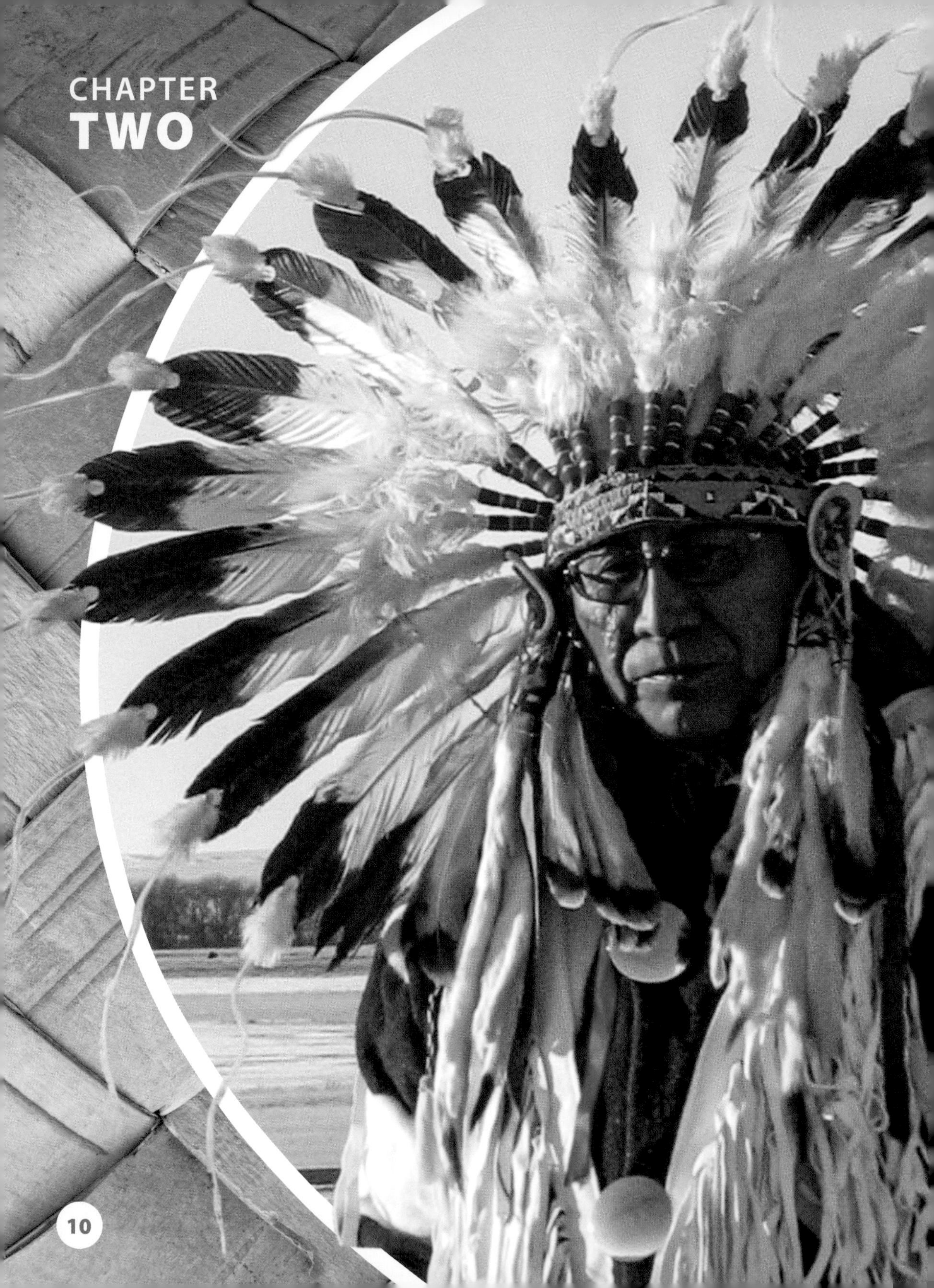

ALL MY RELATIONS

The Lakota use the phrase "all my relations" to explain the way they see the world. It means that everyone and everything on Earth are related. This includes not only people and animals, but also trees, grass, rivers, and mountains. Many Plains Nations share this view of the world. It can be seen in stories, dances, and ceremonies.

Arvol Looking Horse, a Lakota man, participates in a ceremony linking the Lakota people to buffalo.

PERSPECTIVES

BISON

Bison, also known as buffalo, are important to the Plains people. Before European settlers wiped out nearly all the bison, the Plains people relied on these animals. They used the meat for food, the hides for clothing and homes, and the bones for tools. Horns and hides were also used in sacred ceremonies. Bison were a key food source. There were several methods for hunting bison. Two of these methods were driving them into a corral or stampeding them over a cliff. Their meat would be dried, pounded, and mixed with berries and bison fat to make pemmican. Bison migrated from season to season. Many mobile, nomadic nations followed them for food. Today the US government allows limited hunting of bison.

CREATION STORIES

A creation story explains how the world was formed. Each Plains Nation has stories of this type. Many stories talk about a great flood. They describe how animals worked together to create the world. The Cree, Crow (Apsaalooke), Siksika, and other nations have stories with a character climbing a tree or building a raft to escape the flood.

PLAINS
NATIONS

This map shows the general locations of several Plains Nations and peoples. What do you notice about the extent of the Plains region? How might life in the southern nations differ from life in the northern nations?

CANADA

Alberta

Manitoba

Saskatchewan

Plains Cree

Plains Ojibwa (Saulteaux)

Lake Winnipeg

Ontario

Siksika

Blackfoot **Gros Ventre**

Montana

North Dakota

Minnesota

Lake Superior

Mandan

Crow

Teton **Lakota**

Pawnee **Dakota**

Wisconsin

Lake Michigan

Lake Huron

Michigan

South Dakota

Idaho

Wyoming

Utah

Nebraska **Pawnee**

Iowa

Iowa

Illinois

Indiana

Colorado

Arapaho **Missouri**

Kansas

Missouri

Arizona

New Mexico

Oklahoma

Arkansas

Comanche **Wichita**

Texas

Great herds of bison once covered North America's plains.

Then he asks animals to dive into the water to find
material to make the world. Many animals try and fail.
In Cree versions of the story, a muskrat finally dives in
and brings back mud or sand to help make Earth. In
Crow, Cheyenne (Tsistsistas), and Arapaho versions, a
duck brings up the mud. For the Gros Ventre (A'aninin),

a turtle does it. In a Lakota story, a great eagle rescues a young woman during a flood.

Creation tales also explain how people came to live on the Great Plains. The Lakota people tell a story of how the White Buffalo Woman taught them many things. She first appeared to two hunters as a beautiful

PERSPECTIVES

BUFFALO AND CORN

The importance of the buffalo to the Plains Nations can be seen in their stories. Many stories include finding or hunting buffalo. In one Cheyenne story, two young men dressed in buffalo robes went to a natural spring. They found an old woman who fed them meat and corn from two pots. They ate their fill, but her pots were still full. She gave them the meat and corn to take to their people. She then pointed to the south. They saw large herds of buffalo. She pointed to the north, where they saw vast fields of corn.

woman. One knew her to be a sacred person. She told him that he should go and prepare his people for a visit from her. She blessed the people and gave them a sacred white pipe to use. She taught them seven ways to pray. When she left, she turned into a buffalo of different colors, finally becoming a white buffalo. Many Lakota believe white buffalo are sacred.

White buffalo are considered sacred in several Native American religions.

CHAPTER
THREE

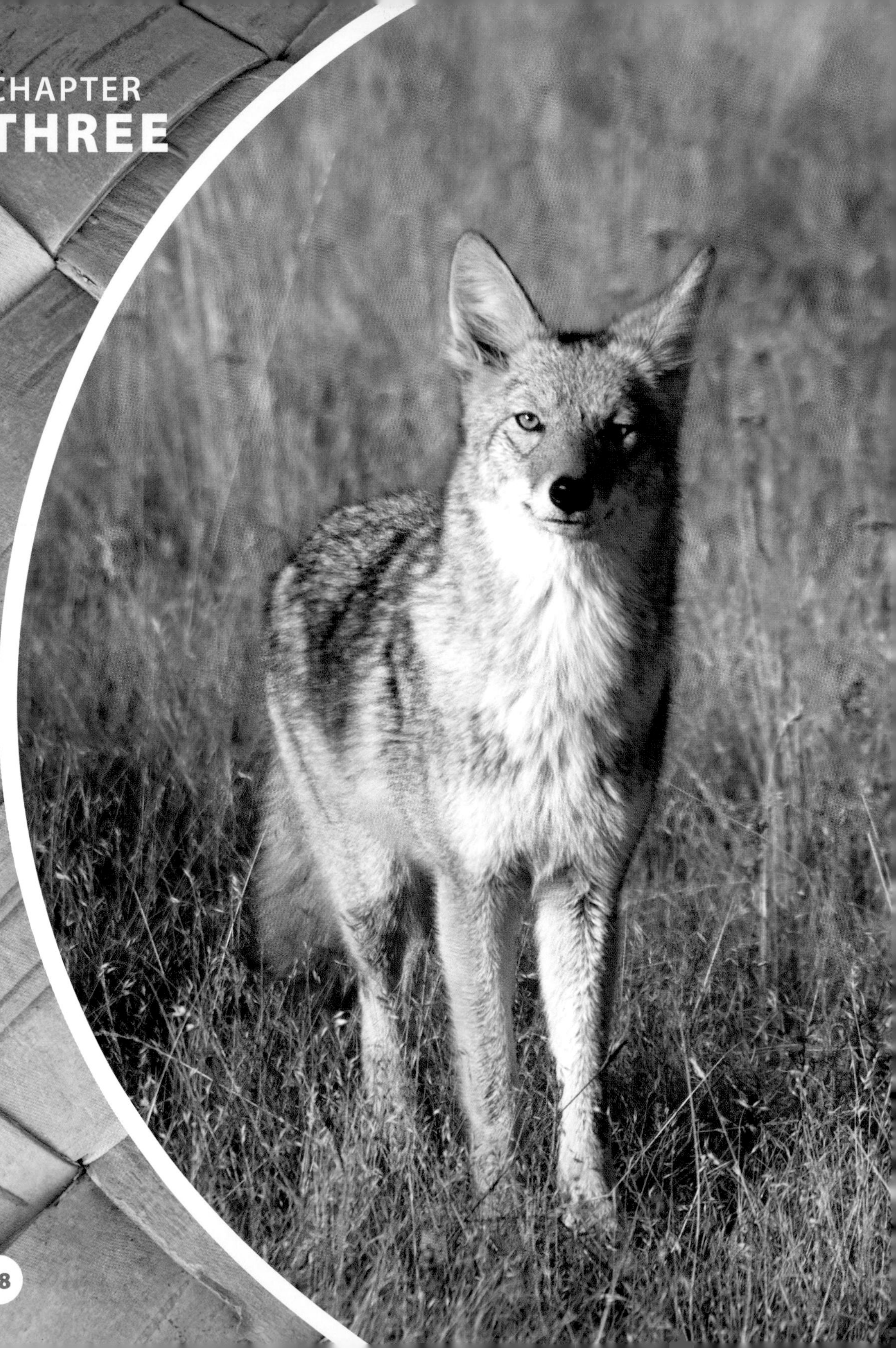

TRICKSTERS, HEROES, AND OTHER CHARACTERS

One character often involved in creation stories is the trickster. The trickster is a powerful character who can be a human, an animal, and a spirit at the same time. Because the stories are sacred, many Plains Nations believe some stories should only be told in certain places at certain times. Stories about the trickster are often told in the winter.

The coyote, a common animal across the Great Plains, is often featured in stories as a trickster.

TRICKSTER TALES

Tricksters have many powers. They can change shape, help people and animals, or even create life. The Spider, Rabbit, and Coyote are common tricksters.

Coyote is the most popular trickster. He can teach and help people, but he can also brag and be greedy. In some stories, Coyote creates the sun and moon or steals them away from someone else. In an Apache story, Coyote finds buffalo being held in a corral by a powerful being. He transforms

TRICKY CHARACTERS

The trickster can appear in many forms and by many names. The Siksika call him Old Man, or Napi. The Crow call him Old Man Coyote. The Lakota call him Iktomi, or Spider-Man. The Cree call the trickster Wisakedjak. In Cree stories, Wisakedjak may be a wolverine, weasel, or coyote. To the Gros Ventre he is known as Nixant. To the Algonquin people he is Nanabozho.

A performer wears traditional clothing from the Gros Ventre Nation, including a coyote head covering, during a ceremony.

himself into a pet for the being's son. Then he tricks his way into the pen. He lets the buffalo out so the people can have food.

HEROES AND OTHER CHARACTERS

The hero in a Plains story can be more than one character. These characters may be animals and people at different times. For example, in one Cree-Métis story, a moose family talks, lives in a lodge, and sleeps in beds. But the next day they are hunted as food.

The moon, by far the brightest object in the night sky, plays a role in many traditional Plains Nations stories.

Animals can play complicated roles in traditional stories, sometimes as characters who can talk or as characters who are hunted.

Many heroes are orphans. Others are poor or disfigured, such as Scar-Face of the Siksika. Heroes may have supernatural powers or get help from those who do. By bravery or by helping others, a hero may regain his family or earn a reward.

In one Siksika story, Long Arrow was an outcast and orphaned deaf boy. At first he cried. When he returned to his tribe, he regained his hearing. A good man adopted him. Long Arrow worked hard and gained acceptance by the tribe. But he wanted to do more. His father blessed him and sent him to search for a horse, also called an elk-dog, from a magical lake. Long Arrow demonstrated his bravery to the lake spirits. For his bravery, Long Arrow was shown how to ride the elk-dogs. He earned gifts to bring back to his father. One gift was a herd of elk-dogs.

EXPLORE ONLINE

Chapter Three discusses the characters that appear in Plains Nations stories. They often take the form of animals. The website below discusses characters that appear in Siksika oral traditions. Which characters are animals? How does their status as animals affect the stories?

GLENBOW MUSEUM: TRADITIONAL STORIES
abdocorelibrary.com/plains-nations

CHAPTER
FOUR

LINKS TO THE LAND

The stories of the Plains Nations say that these people were created on the Great Plains and have always lived there. Scientists have found evidence that people have lived in this region for thousands of years. The tribes' stories tell of changes in the landscape and how rivers or mountains were formed.

Europeans brought horses to the Great Plains in the 1600s. Siksika stories tell how the new animals changed their lives. Horses meant

Horses remain a part of many Plains Nations people's lives today.

more freedom to travel. They also took over dogs' previous job of pulling a travois full of goods.

AN ANCHOR IN CHANGING TIMES

Until the late 1800s, the Plains people had land, food, water, wood for fires, and game for hunting and supplies. Powerful nations, such as the Cree and Lakota, then began to widen their territory and push others out. Europeans also began to move into the Great Plains region in greater numbers. They created more conflict.

Throughout these changes, storytellers used stories to help reinforce traditions and explain the world around them. One example of this is the Siksika story of Star-Boy. He was the son of Morning Star, or the planet Venus, and a Siksika woman. The Siksika woman journeyed to the sky on the Spider-Man's web through the North Star, which was a hole in the heavens. She later returned to her village.

To win a wife, her son Star-Boy went back to the sky world. The Sun taught him the Sun Dance and other

Some Plains Nations stories are built around the people's observations of the planets and stars.

traditions. Then Star-Boy returned to teach these to the Siksika. Now Star-Boy, or the planet Jupiter, rises first. He is followed by his father, Morning Star, and then his grandfather, the Sun.

BUFFALO RANGE

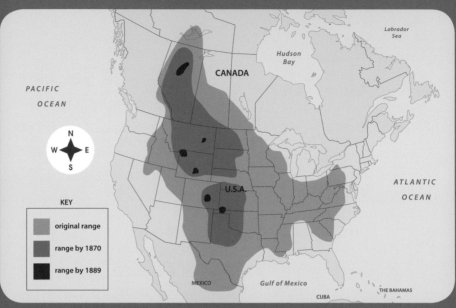

In the late 1800s, US settlers killed millions of buffalo on the Great Plains. This map shows how the range of the buffalo shrank during this time. Why would the buffalo have been such a useful animal to the Native Nations? And how would this major change affect these people?

HUNTING OR FARMING?

The Plains people usually followed the buffalo and relied on hunting. However, they also planted crops such as squash, corn, and beans. A story from the Mandan people tells that seeing the geese return in spring meant it was time to plant corn. Seeing swans meant squash, and seeing ducks meant beans.

Corn was growing in Mexico at least 7,000 years ago. More than 150 types of corn were being grown in North America before the arrival of Europeans. The nations that grew corn would farm and control it in specific ways to develop the different types. Corn was also traded. The Plains tribes who didn't grow corn traded for it and relied on it in their diet.

CORN LEGENDS

An Arikara story begins with one young hunter who watched a lone buffalo for four days. Each day it stood by itself in one spot, facing a different direction. Then it was gone. Where it stood, he found its tracks and a strange plant. But there were no tracks leading to or from it. He told his people. They watched the plant flower and ripen. The young man touched it and found red corn called maize. The people divided the kernels and grew it. They had such a good harvest that they invited other tribes to share it. From then on, corn was grown by many nations.

MAKING TREATIES

White settlers and Native Americans made many peace treaties in the 1800s as a way to avoid fighting and wars.

TREATIES

In Canada, 11 numbered treaties negotiated from 1871 to 1921 are still used. In 1876, almost 2,000 Cree, Assiniboine, and Saulteaux people gathered to talk about Treaty 6. Talks went on for several days. One Native American leader said, "This is our land, it isn't a piece of pemmican to be cut off and given in little pieces back to us." However, the tribes were able to negotiate a few positive things from the government: medical care and the promise of help in times of famine.

However, the settlers often violated the treaties. In the late 1800s, US settlers killed millions of buffalo. They left the animals' bodies to rot on the plains. Plains Nations were left starving.

During treaty negotiations, the Plains Nations often spoke using allegories, or stories with hidden meanings. They also discussed everything carefully before they made a decision. During treaty talks, the tribes' people paid attention to every word spoken. Even years later, they could repeat what each side said, word for word.

STRAIGHT TO THE
SOURCE

Some people of the Plains Nations have told stories through artwork. A 2016 museum exhibit featured some of this art. An introduction to the exhibit reads:

Warrior-artists from the Native nations of North America's plains have long practiced a pictorial style of illustration. This dynamic tradition began with depictions of visionary experiences. Men also painted buffalo-hide tipis, robes and shirts to record their successes in battle and horse raiding. In the 1800s, Native artists began to use pencils, crayons, canvas, muslin and paper. Although the materials were new, their reasons for painting and drawing initially did not change. . . . Since the 1960s, narrative artists have freely blended traditional and modern materials to depict everything from ceremonies and family histories to humor and contemporary life.

Source: "Unbound: Narrative Art of the Plains." *Newsdesk.* Smithsonian, March 1, 2016. Web. Accessed December 15, 2016.

Consider Your Audience

Write a blog post adapting this passage about the history of Plains Nations art for a new audience, such as a classmate. How does your blog post differ from the original text?

CHAPTER
FIVE

WHAT WILL THE FUTURE HOLD?

The stories of the people of the Plains hold value today. Singing, dancing, and storytelling continue to be important in the lives of many peoples. Today, storytelling is featured in many powwows at special events held across North America. When, where, and why a story is told also hold meaning for storytellers and listeners. To the Plains peoples, these stories are about more than legendary creatures and events.

The people of the Plains Nations still value traditions that their nations have maintained for many generations.

MODERN POWWOWS

Ojibwa, Cree, and other peoples hold a tradition known as the powwow. The events are frequently held in the spring and summer, though some also happen in the fall and winter. People share stories, culture, art, and dance. The popular Hoop Dance is a form of storytelling in which the dancer forms shapes with hoops. The shapes include butterflies, eagles, and snakes. Powwows may last for a few hours or a few days. They bring people together to celebrate their culture.

The stories are a way to tell about their history, lives, and experiences today.

COURTS AND LEGISLATION

In land claims and court cases, courts tend to trust physical or written evidence. Someone's memory of what was said during treaty talks is not considered as reliable as the written words of a treaty. Nations' oral histories were first accepted in courtrooms in 1997. That year, the Supreme Court of Canada ruled that oral history must be treated as equal to other forms of historical evidence. In sentencing circles, people are asked to "speak from the heart" to help offenders make amends to victims. Similar systems are sometimes used in the United States.

SEEKING JUSTICE

In 2005, survivors of Indian Residential Schools sued the Canadian government. For more than 100 years, the government had forced First Nations children into schools far from their families. They were not allowed to speak their languages or follow their traditions. Many suffered abuse. The survivors wanted compensation for this treatment.

PERSPECTIVES
THE WORLD OF THE WHITE BUFFALO

The Lakota believe the white buffalo stories and prophecies have a special meaning in the modern world. They keep the sacred pipe that the White Buffalo Woman brought them. Traditionally, the appearance of a white buffalo means all people must come together and live in peace. Modern storytellers connect this theme to today's dangers, such as climate change.

In 2008, Canadian prime minister Stephen Harper, *right*, met with Native American leaders and offered an official apology for abuse at the Indian Residential Schools.

During the investigation, people talked about the stories they had heard in their childhood and how important that was for them. Their testimony showed how they had been hurt and abused by the experience.

On June 11, 2008, the prime minister of Canada, Stephen Harper, formally apologized. The government set up a fund to give $1.9 billion in Canadian dollars to the 80,000 survivors. Today, government budgets set aside money to help indigenous communities.

THE STORIES OF THE PLAINS

Like all cultures, the Native Nations of the Great Plains tell stories for many reasons. Some stories explain the creation of the world. Others tell about the creatures and beings behind everyday events. Passed-down stories about abuse at Native boarding schools are helping people find justice. All of these types of stories hold value and importance to the Plains Nations.

FURTHER EVIDENCE

This book has discussed the white buffalo prophecy and its importance to the Plains people. Some believe it is important to all people. Visit the below website, and watch the video. What does the white buffalo mean to Chief Arvol Looking Horse? What does the message mean to you? How could you help?

CHIEF ARVOL LOOKING HORSE
SPEAKS OF WHITE BUFFALO PROPHECY
abdocorelibrary.com/plains-nations

Residential school survivors participated in emotional events at which stories from the past were shared.

STORY
SUMMARIES

The White Buffalo Woman (Lakota)

The White Buffalo Woman story tells of a spiritual figure who visited the Lakota to bring the gift of a pipe and her teachings. She became a white buffalo calf as she left. The Lakota believe the presence of a white buffalo means all peoples must come together and live in peace.

Coyote, the Trickster (Apache)

Creation stories for Plains Nations often involve a trickster, such as Coyote. In one story, Coyote finds a buffalo being held in a corral. Using trickery, he is able to release the buffalo so that the people can have food.

Oral Histories and Justice

Oral histories have been used to remember traditional ways, to get justice in the courts, to get the Canadian government to apologize for injustices, and to help rebuild the position of various First Nations and Native American people in Canada and the United States.

STOP AND
THINK

Tell the Tale

Chapter Four discusses stories based on the stars and planets visible in the night sky. Creating stories about the night sky is common in cultures all around the world. Look up at the night sky and write 200 words about what you see. Why might the night sky be such a common canvas for telling stories?

Surprise Me

This book discusses Plains storytellers and the way they tell stories. After reading this book, what two or three facts about storytelling or storytellers did you find most surprising? Write a few sentences about each fact. Why did you find each fact surprising?

Why Do I Care?

Storytelling is used for many purposes. It shares cultural traditions, teaches moral lessons, and provides entertainment. What kinds of stories do you experience in your daily life? What purposes do they serve?

You Are There

This book discusses the influence of stories on treaties between Native Americans and governments. Imagine you are a witness at a treaty negotiation. Write a letter home telling your friends what you saw and heard. What do you notice about the different peoples and nations attending? Be sure to add plenty of detail to your notes.

GLOSSARY

allegory
a kind of story that uses symbols, characters, and events to reveal a deeper meaning or lesson

compensation
payment made in recognition of wrongdoing

migrate
to move from one region to another

nomadic
mobile and moving from place to place, often following game or seasons

pemmican
buffalo meat that is pounded and mixed with buffalo fat and berries

travois
a kind of sled with long poles, pulled by a dog or horse

treaty
a formal agreement between two nations

trickster
a spirit being with supernatural powers who plays tricks and also helps people

LEARN MORE

Books

Indian Nations of North America. Washington, DC: National Geographic, 2010.

Taylor, C. J. *All the Stars in the Sky: Native Stories from the Heavens.* Plattsburgh, NY: Tundra Books, 2006.

Yasuda, Anita. *American Bison.* Minneapolis, MN: Abdo Publishing, 2017.

Websites

To learn more about Native American Oral Histories, visit **abdobooklinks.com**. These links are routinely monitored and updated to provide the most current information available.

Visit **abdocorelibrary.com** for free additional tools for teachers and students.

INDEX

About the Author

Marie Powell lives in Treaty 4 land, in Regina, Saskatchewan. She has written more than 35 children's books and two young adult novels. Her favorite subjects to write about are science, history, and storytelling.